Original title:
The Andromeda Affair

Copyright © 2025 Creative Arts Management OÜ
All rights reserved.

Author: Harris Montgomery
ISBN HARDBACK: 978-1-80567-837-3
ISBN PAPERBACK: 978-1-80567-958-5

Starlight Serenade

In the sky, a dancing light,
A cat on a comet took flight.
Socks on his paws, he zoomed through space,
Chasing aliens in a wild race.

Wobbling planets hopped by in cheer,
Joking asteroids, what a funny sphere!
With giggles of stars, they twinkled bright,
Echoing laughter, a cosmic delight.

Dust and Dreams

A dreamer launched with props on a broom,
Swept up stardust, who turned into gloom.
The Milky Way giggled at his clumsy flight,
While a dwarf planet offered him some light.

He spiraled past a moon made of cheese,
With mice in spacesuits, oh, what a tease!
Each crumb floated, a tasty surprise,
As he let out a laugh that covered the skies.

Celestial Convergence

Two stars collided, a sparkly mess,
Cosmic confetti that wore a red dress.
They twirled and danced, a ball in the void,
Inviting all comets, none to be coyed.

The universe chuckled, what a grand show!
With black holes spinning, putting on a glow.
Even the aliens rolled on the ground,
As laughter encircled and joy was found.

Galactic Promises

A promise was made by a starry brigade,
To make constellations, a comical parade.
With twinkling giggles in every design,
They painted the night with laughter divine.

Jupiter winked with a smile so broad,
While Saturn's rings danced, how very odd!
They promised each night to light up the way,
And share silly stories until break of day.

Love in the Twilight

In the dusk we dance and twirl,
With cosmic jokes that make us whirl.
Aliens laugh with silly grins,
As we swap our interstellar sins.

Floating past the planet's rings,
We joke about the oddest things.
With every comet's zany flight,
Our love glows bright in fading light.

Celestial Kaleidoscope

Colors clash in cosmic play,
While meteors zoom, we laugh away.
Your bright smile in the starry sea,
Is like a comet coming free.

Juggling asteroids and shooting stars,
We make wishes on our silly cars.
With every laugh a galaxy spins,
Creating worlds where love begins.

Haunting Crescendo of Light

Echoes of laughter fill the air,
With ghostly stars that float with flair.
We chase the shadows, hand in hand,
Finding joy in the ghostly land.

Witty whispers from the moon,
As we waltz to a haunting tune.
In this eerie, fun-filled night,
Our love's a blaze, a thrilling fright.

Starlit Longing

Beneath the sky of sparkling treasures,
We find delight in wild pleasures.
Your giggle resonates through space,
A sound that time cannot erase.

With every twinkle, every sigh,
We craft our dreams to the stars up high.
In the night, we sing and play,
Starlit wishes on display.

Celestial Secrets

In a galaxy far, but so near,
Aliens joke with laughter and cheer.
Fumbling with their shiny gadgets,
They spill their drinks, oh what bad habits!

Spaceships zoom with twists and turns,
While Martians play with lunar urns.
Planets dance a cosmic jig,
Adventures start with a little dig!

Asteroids ring like silly bells,
Their antics echo in cosmic swells.
Comets trail with a wink and grin,
This is where the laughs begin!

So look up high, you might just see,
Silly beings sipping cosmic tea.
In the universe, funny things abound,
In every starlit nook, joy is found!

Whispering Stars

Whispering stars with laughter bright,
Giggle softly in the night.
They tell tales of clumsy moons,
And dancing suns to silly tunes.

Nebulas puff like cotton candy,
While cosmic clowns juggle so dandy.
The Milky Way is a twinkling stage,
Where every quasar acts their age.

Wormholes giggle when things go wrong,
Carrying ships where they don't belong.
Black holes chuckle as they munch,
On cosmic snacks during lunch.

So listen close when you gaze above,
For the universe teems with playful love.
Stars laugh and tease, oh what a sight,
In the grand cosmic playhouse of night!

Love Among the Nebulae

In the nebulae where giggles bloom,
Two comets swoon in a starry room.
Their trails twinkle with each sweet kiss,
Floating through space, such cosmic bliss!

Asteroids flirt with a playful nudge,
While over there, a black hole will judge.
'Are they dating or just making plans?'
Ask the cosmic squirrels, they know the fans!

Stars align for this love so grand,
Holding hands in a galactic band.
Planets cheer and shoot their confetti,
Delighting in the love that's heartfelt and petty.

So laugh in the light of a billion spheres,
For cosmic love conquers all our fears.
In the vastness, let your heart beam,
Among the gas clouds, we all can dream!

Echoes of Distant Worlds

Echoes of laughter from worlds afar,
Reaching our ears from a bright green star.
Where creatures dance with jiggly legs,
And serve up drinks in alien kegs.

Silly beings with three fuzzy eyes,
Play peek-a-boo behind cosmic pies.
Whimsical laughter fills the void,
In the cosmos, worries are all destroyed.

Planets throw a raucous bash,
While rockets roll in a speedy dash.
Gravity's just a playful tease,
As all creation flows with ease.

So venture forth, feel the fun unfold,
In distant realms, where tales are told.
Echoes of joy in the vast expanse,
Invite us all to join the dance!

Chasing Infinity

In a ship made of cheese, we zoom through the dark,
Dodging space squirrels, giving them quite a lark.
With our snacks floating by in the weightless delight,
We laugh at the stars, oh what a silly sight.

Planets spin in circles, a dance of pure glee,
One twirls with a hula hoop, just wait and you'll see.
But watch out for comets, they're speedy and loud,
Crashing our party, oh, we'll say it aloud!

Time flies like a vacuum, it's bold and it's brave,
Running from gravity's joke, oh the mess that we save!
With laughter as fuel, we ride on this quest,
Chasing infinity, we're dressed in our best.

Dreams of a Dying Star

A star with a wig dreams of glittery trends,
She's throwing a party, inviting her friends.
With supernova balloons and cosmic confetti,
The light show starts early, isn't it pretty?

But wait! What's this? She feels a bit chubby,
A stardust diet could fix her old tubby.
Yet her friends cheer her on, with cake made of rays,
Laughing and tumbling in stellar displays.

As they dance to the rhythm of galactic beats,
A black hole crashes in, stealing all the sweets.
But laughter and joy are the best kind of scars,
So they twirl round the void, our glorious stars.

Unraveling Cosmic Threads

In a tangle of yarn, the cosmos unspools,
Tiny aliens knitting, confounding our rules.
With needles of light and a thimble of gloom,
They craft us a blanket to cover the room.

But one little stitch, it broke with a pop,
And chaos erupted, oh what a great flop!
Galaxies tangled in loops and in spins,
Cackling together, oh how the fun begins!

They patch it with laughter, a cosmic repair,
Adding a pocket for snacks, because who would dare?
So next time you wonder about that night sky,
Remember the aliens, as time flutters by.

Midnight in the Milky Way

At midnight we gather, for a celestial snack,
Milky Way bars and stardust, we'll never look back.
Under the glow of the giant moon pie,
We tell silly stories, and watch the stars fly.

Meteor showers bring wishes and cheer,
Each wishing for pizza, or maybe a beer.
The planets all giggle, they know what we want,
A universe feast on the endless front lawn.

With laughter as bright as a thousand suns,
We dance in the moonlight, just having our fun.
So if you hear giggles from the sky up above,
It's just us in orbit, sharing our love.

Cosmic Threads

In the space of silly dreams,
Aliens dance in cosmic beams.
With wobbly legs and quirky hats,
They trip on stars and giggle, chitchat.

Planets spin in a merry chase,
Shooting stars don't know their place.
They whizz past moons in a dizzy whirl,
Calling all comets for a wild twirl.

Galaxies knit with laughter's thread,
While robots joke about the bread.
A universe dressed in mismatched wear,
Where space-time bends with joyful flair.

So raise a glass of cosmic cheer,
To those who float without a fear.
In this funny, vast expanse above,
We find the quirks we truly love.

Intergalactic Tales

Once a spaceship tried to bake,
But forgot to set the steerage shake.
It floated off with cookies galore,
A sweet surprise from the cosmic store!

Martians playing hide and seek,
In black holes that are far from bleak.
They sneak and peek, oh what a sight,
Bumping into stars in sheer delight.

Asteroids roll with laughter loud,
Forming a comet, quite proud.
In this raucous, cosmic parade,
Every twist and turn's a charade!

The rocket's engine puffed and snorted,
As space pirates whimpered, 'We're thwarted!'
Yet in this far-off stellar zone,
Laughter rings, as jesters have grown.

Eclipsed by the Night

Underneath a darkened sky,
A space cow mooed, oh my, oh my!
With a twinkle and a wink so bright,
It played tag with the moon last night.

The stars all danced in a funky show,
While meteors spun, putting on a glow.
Planets laughed in a merry fight,
As they juggled comets with all their might.

A black hole hiccuped, lose its pace,
Slurping matter like a sweet embrace.
While Saturn's rings jingled like bells,
Every echo shared a galaxy of yells.

So let's tiptoe through the cosmic puns,
Where even space gives out fun runs.
In this night of raucous delight,
The universe beams, eclipsed with light.

Constellations of the Heart

Love blooms in a stellar park,
Where comets chase and rocket from dark.
A Venus star spans candy skies,
While Moonbeam winks with twinkling eyes.

Jupiter hums a romantic tune,
While teasing the sunlit afternoons.
With Martian blushes and lunar hugs,
They share sweet whispers, cosmic mugs.

In this dance of planets and dreams,
Galaxies swirl like ice cream streams.
A universe stitched with giggles and glee,
Where even the dark has a jubilee.

So orbit close, oh lovers dear,
In this grand space, there's naught to fear.
With hearts that twinkle like stars above,
We'll write our tales in the heavens of love.

In the Wake of Celestial Storms

When comets clash in cosmic dance,
Galaxies swirl in a goofy prance.
Aliens giggle with green balloon hats,
As they serve up tea with cosmic splats.

Stars twinkle bright in the lemonade skies,
While asteroids tumble, stumbling like spies.
Planets wobble in jovial fright,
Singing karaoke, a celestial night.

Space cows moo in zero-gravity glee,
Chasing black holes like they're chasing a bee.
With each twirl and spin, they misbehave,
In this cosmic circus, we're all a bit brave.

So toast to the stars with a fizzy delight,
In the wake of storms, all is just right.
With laughter and joy, together we soar,
In this universe, who could ask for more?

Veils of Light and Shades of Love

In nebulae veils, we find our finesse,
Floating on stardust, we never digress.
Rocket ships whizzing like bees on a spree,
While love notes drift on the cosmic sea.

Shooting stars wink, giving quirky advice,
To kiss chomping comets? Oh, that's really nice!
Jupiter chuckles, it's quite the affair,
With twinkling romances, floating in air.

Galactic laughter fills spaces so wide,
As we wear our heart-shaped helmets with pride.
Moonbeams giggle, "Is that love, I see?"
Yes, my dear friend, it's you and me!

So dance in the orbits, let joy intertwine,
With veils of light where our hearts align.
Beyond the horizons, let silly things swoop,
In shades of affection, forever we loop.

A Dance of Light in the Dark Abyss

In shadows deep, a party brews,
Galactic beings with silly shoes.
They twirl and spin, a cosmic sight,
With rubber ducks that glow at night.

A comet's tail, they ride with glee,
Swapping tales of space and tea.
With every step, a starlit laugh,
Who knew the void could host a chaff?

A meteorite takes flight and slips,
Landing right on a martian's hips.
They giggle round the dark, so bright,
In this wild waltz of the twilight flight.

Each twinkle shared is pure delight,
As aliens dance till morning light.
In the abyss, they're quite the show,
Not a black hole, but a cosmic glow.

Fragments of Stardust Dreams

In dreams of dust, they trip and fall,
A nebula fluffs up, oh what a ball!
A space cat juggles moons and stars,
While aliens race in little cars.

With cosmic pies that float and spin,
They munch on clouds with goofy grins.
Galactic giggles fill the night,
In this dreamscape that feels just right.

Asteroids bounce like giant balls,
As they laugh and play in warp-speed stalls.
Then someone rockets off to space,
And comes back home with a toaster face.

Each dream a riddle, each laugh a flop,
They chase the echoes, then they stop.
In fragments bright, their giggles gleam,
Stardust glows in this wild dream.

Embers of Love in Cosmic Currents

In swirling hues, a couple spins,
Dodging meteors and playful winds.
With flirtatious winks that warp the air,
They whisper sweet nothings to stray comets fair.

Across the stars, their laughter streams,
As they toast to life with milky creams.
Galaxies twirl in swirling flight,
Yet it's their giggles that feel just right.

On solar sails, they cruise with flair,
With ice cream cones and stellar care.
Each flicker of love, a cosmic tease,
As they dance through space with elegant ease.

Embers flicker in the starlit void,
With playful sparks, their hearts are buoyed.
In this universe, strange but true,
Love's a cosmic joke shared by two.

Celestial Cartography of the Heart

With maps of stars and hearts in tow,
They chart the skies where wild dreams flow.
A cosmic guide with charts and lines,
Leads to bizarre love that intertwines.

Through nebulas and comets bright,
They navigate with sheer delight.
Each heartbeat echoes a cosmic sound,
In the universe of love unbound.

They slip through asteroids, oh what fun,
With laughter loud, they're never done.
Mapping love in orbits awry,
Two souls collide in the sapphire sky.

Celestial dreams spiral high above,
Sketching the equinox of love.
In every twist, their hearts engrave,
A map of laughter across the wave.

Stars Beneath the Surface

In a galaxy far, odd things reside,
Space squirrels take their morning glide.
They gather snacks from cosmic trees,
Nibbling stardust with such ease.

Their laughter echoes through the night,
Chasing stars that twinkle bright.
Planets wobble, joining in fun,
A space race 'round a giant sun.

Asteroids dance, a wild disco,
Galactic boogie, don't you know?
Aliens prance in pointy shoes,
While comets stumble, sharing news.

So if you gaze at skies so bold,
Remember tales of shapes untold.
The universe, a wacky place,
Where every star wears a silly face.

Time's Cosmic Canvas

In the halls of time, clocks go 'ding',
Planets trade their celestial bling.
A comet sneezes, a supernova coughs,
Quantum cats play peek-a-boo in soft troves.

When moons overcook their crescent pies,
Gravity giggles as stardust flies.
Time travelers trip over their own feet,
Creating funny ripples, oh so sweet.

A wormhole whispers jokes from the past,
While time's canvas splashes colors fast.
The future's a canvas yet to be drawn,
With lines that twist from dusk till dawn.

So dance with time, but beware of fate,
Make sure your watch is not too late.
In this cosmic jest, we all play a role,
Painting the cosmos with a giggling soul.

Celestial Reflections

Mirrors in space reflect our dreams,
Where stars chuckle over moonbeams.
Galaxies peek, curious and bright,
Whispering secrets in the quiet night.

A meteor shower, a glittery prank,
Dancing droplets in space's tank.
Nebulas swirl with colors so free,
Making cosmic art for all to see.

When planets play hopscotch without a care,
Creating ripples in the cosmic air.
Starlight flickers, stars play coy,
In a universe filled with interstellar joy.

So gaze into the night, share a laugh,
For cosmic reflections are the best half.
In starlit embraces, we'll forever dwell,
Where humour beams through the astral shell.

Veils of the Milky Way

In the folds of space, laughter flits,
Where milk from the Milky Way drips.
Cosmic cows mooooo, dancing with grace,
Creating a ruckus in this vast space.

Stars hide beneath their leafy veils,
Sipping juice from comet's tails.
Galactic tourists snap silly pics,
While space whales perform their tricks.

UFOs zoom, playing tag in the dark,
While black holes sit, ready to spark.
Aliens laugh, reading silly signs,
Trying to decipher Earth's naughty lines.

So hang your hat on a shooting star,
Join the fun from near or far.
When veils of wonder swirl and sway,
The universe giggles in its own way.

Whispers in the Galaxy

In a world where aliens dance,
They argue over pizza, what a chance!
One claims pineapple's a crime,
While the other says it's just sublime.

Stars giggle as comets race,
A jelly bean in outer space!
With laughter bouncing off each star,
They wonder if they've gone too far.

Black holes hoot and swirl in glee,
While meteors sip cosmic tea.
Rockets zoom, and aliens cheer,
Next stop: the annual space fair!

So if you catch a starry wink,
Just know it's more than you might think!
For in this vast and funny scene,
The universe is quite serene!

Beyond the Cosmic Veil

Beyond a veil of twinkling light,
Space bugs dance, a hilarious sight!
They wear their hats, not made of hats,
But flying saucers, oh how they chat!

Galactic critters paint in hues,
Of pinkish green and crazy blues.
They giggle as they send a tweet,
To Martians, offering some sweets.

Planets bounce in jovial tunes,
While astronauts juggle with the moons.
A cosmic pie, now that's a dream,
To share with friends, the universe's theme!

So peek beyond the starry stream,
Where laughter flows, and dreamers beam.
It's fun out here, among the best,
In a cosmic game, you're the guest.

Tales from the Stars

Once upon a time in space,
A starfish won a dancing race!
With twinkling lights upon its feet,
It boogied to a funky beat.

Asteroids had a rock band fun,
Their solo act? The super sun!
In orbits tight, they played all night,
Till supernova took the spotlight.

A comet who dreamed to paint the sky,
Mixed colors that made planets sigh.
With swirls and sparks, a vibrant cheer,
Who knew space was so sincere?

So gather 'round, my cosmic friends,
For every tale, the fun transcends.
In this vast realm, the laughs ignite,
With every star, a joyful light!

A Cosmic Love Story

In the void where lovebirds sing,
An alien asked a star for bling.
With meteor showers for romance's spark,
They danced 'til dawn, a cosmic lark!

She wore her best meteoric gown,
He found a rocket for a crown.
Together they spun in blissful glee,
While space whales hummed their harmony.

Galaxies glowed, oh what a sight,
As lovebugs soared through the endless night.
Their laughter twinkled, bright and bold,
In tales that the universe has told.

So let's toast to this cosmic pair,
For love in space is quite rare!
With every wink from distant stars,
They've made their mark among the czars!

Celestial Resonance

In outer space, a cat plays tricks,
With asteroids, using cosmic sticks.
Aliens giggle, they can't believe,
As black holes dance, and space-time weaves.

Neptune wears a silly hat,
While Saturn's rings hold a giant bat.
The stars wink like they've had some wine,
And comets want to join the line.

Astro-nuts float with peanut shells,
Sharing puns that ring like bells.
Galaxies spin, a merry band,
With cosmic jokes that never land.

In this realm where laughter roams,
Even light beams call it home.
So lift your glass to the great unknown,
Join the laughter, you're not alone.

Lost in Space and Time

A rocket ship lost its GPS,
Wandered past Mars in quite a mess.
An alien waved, said, "You're quite late!"
"Join my conga line, it'll be great!"

Planets took selfies with silly poses,
While moons giggled, hiding their noses.
A space-time hiccup caused quite a fuss,
As astronauts danced, full of trust.

A time machine broke; oh what a sight!
Dinosaurs joined the moonlit night.
"We'll have a party!" was the loud cheer,
As meteors whizzed, bringing strange beer.

Stellar hijinks, a cosmic spree,
In a universe, wild and free.
So if you're lost, just spin and twirl,
You might discover a whole new world!

Voyage of the Celestials

A ship of stars sailed through the void,
Captain Bunny was quite overjoyed.
With jellybeans for fuel, they set sail,
Navigating through a cosmic tail.

A disco ball hung from the bow,
While aliens danced, "Come join us now!"
Constellations hummed a catchy tune,
As they boogied under a glow of the moon.

Galactic snacks in a floating bowl,
Space fries served without a roll.
"Galactic gossip" was the talk of the night,
As they shared tales of a supernova fight.

With laughter echoing, the stars twinkled bright,
In their voyage through an endless night.
So grab your friends and join the show,
In the universe, let fun overflow!

Distant Horizons

On distant shores of light and sound,
A robot danced with a cat profound.
"Let's name this place Cactus Void!"
As giggles erupted, joy was deployed.

Planets served soda in alien cups,
As space cows floated, doing jumps.
A comet's tail swept, painting the sky,
And the black hole winked as it passed by.

Astronauts traded their helmets for hats,
Saying, "We're serious, but love the spats!"
Cosmic games, through time and space,
Laughter echoes in this boundless place.

So wander far, across the stars bright,
Find humor in every thrilling flight.
In the end, we're all just a part,
Of this universe that tickles the heart.

Interstellar Whispers

In a galaxy not so far,
Aliens played guitar,
They strummed on a comet's tail,
While sipping blue space ale.

The stars danced with delight,
In a cosmic, silly fight,
Planets giggled, rolled around,
In this wacky, vast playground.

A Martian lost his shoe,
Stumbling on a cosmic brew,
He laughed, 'What a clumsy fate!'
As stardust turned to cake.

With each twinkle in the sky,
A supernova's cheeky sigh,
They whispered jokes through the light,
Making shadows burst with fright.

Planets in Motion

Planets twirled in silly dance,
Flirting with a meteor's chance,
Jupiter rolled, Saturn spun,
While Venus tried to out-run.

Mars challenged Earth to a race,
'The red one wins!' was Mars' base,
But Earth took a clever turn,
Leaving the crowd there to yearn.

Asteroids shared some funny tales,
Of finding lost interstellar mails,
While black holes played hide and seek,
Swallowing laughter, oh so sleek.

In this playground of the skies,
No one wanted dull goodbyes,
Stars winked, comets flew by fast,
As the universe chuckled, aghast.

Cosmic Embrace

In space, where the laughter echoes wide,
Cosmic beings take a joyful ride,
A nebula's hug, soft and bright,
Turns black holes to giggly sights.

The moons played hide and seek with suns,
Hiding behind asteroids just for fun,
While supernovae popped in delight,
Creating fireworks through the night.

A quasar grinned with a radiant glow,
Tickling stars in a cosmic show,
Each twinkle told a joke or two,
In this universe where laughter flew.

With every orbit, laughter grew,
Spreading joy in shades of blue,
Cosmic embrace, hilarious and bright,
In the theater of endless night.

Journeys Through the Void

Rocket ships with balloon-like flair,
Traveled through the void without a care,
Captains wore hats, all striped and tall,
As laughter echoed through the space hall.

Aliens with goofy, wild wigs,
Played leapfrog over cosmic jigs,
Exploring black holes' giggling sound,
While starfish danced on stardust ground.

They flew through nebulae full of light,
Sipping stardust smoothies, oh what a sight,
With a wink, they'd launch into a spin,
As the universe cracked up in a grin.

So off they went, on paths unknown,
Finding joy in the space they'd grown,
In this vast, hilarious sea of stars,
Adventures awaited, beyond Mars.

Love Across the Milky Abyss

In a café made of stardust,
A barista with three heads served me drinks,
I spilled coffee on a black hole,
It laughed, and I forgot how to think.

I tried to flirt with a comet,
But it whizzed past and made a quick exit,
Its tail was too bright to handle,
And I guess it just didn't fit.

There were aliens dancing in pairs,
With antennae swaying to unheard beats,
I joined in, twirling with flair,
Till I tripped over cosmic feet.

Love found me in the strangest place,
Where planets wore hats and shoes bright,
In the end, it was all just a chase,
For laughter under the shimmering light.

Shadows in the Spiral's Dance

In the spiral arms of a galaxy so wide,
I met a shadow with two left feet,
We danced through nebulae, and oh, what a ride,
Losing track of an interstellar beat.

The stars giggled at our clumsy sway,
While meteorites whizzed from afar,
Catching our laughter like rays of the day,
Hand in hand, we spun like a shooting star.

A rogue planet joined to steal the show,
And tripped on its own dusty ring,
We burst out laughing, oh what a glow,
As we twirled through the cosmic bling.

In darkness, our silly moves lit the night,
While constellations looked on with a grin,
In this waltz of shadows, everything felt right,
Amidst the chaos, where light and fun begin.

Celestial Reckoning of Lost Souls

A lost soul checked its GPS,
In a realm where maps just don't exist,
It searched and searched without success,
Fell over a comet, and oh, what a twist!

Asteroids played a game of tag,
While I counted stars with a fumble,
Each time I'd slip, my spirit would brag,
That I cracked the cosmos in a tumble.

Ghosts of astronauts danced by the moon,
In spacesuits made of cotton candy,
We twirled and spun to a ludicrous tune,
As supernovas winked, ever so dandy.

In this celestial mess, we found our beat,
Embracing mayhem under starlit skies,
A reckoning not of sorrow, but sweet,
For joy in chaos, as each moment flies.

Interstellar Serenades of Longing

I serenaded a star with a ukulele,
Its twinkling laugh echoed through the void,
We sang of love and pizza, oh so gaily,
Where vacuum space permitted joy, not annoyed.

An asteroid took the role of my muse,
With a knack for rhythm and some cheeky zest,
It suggested we dance, I couldn't refuse,
And so we kicked off a cosmic fest.

A wormhole opened just for our tune,
While astrological signs bobbed their heads,
In this vastness where no one was immune,
Fun erupted like soda, skyward it spreads.

As planets joined in with playful refrain,
And black holes hummed, oh what a delight,
In the strum of the stars, I felt no pain,
Just interstellar serenades, deep into the night.

Celestial Warbles

In the quiet of the night, oh so clear,
Space critters gather, ready for cheer.
Aliens in tutus do a waltz,
While comets chuckle at their silly faults.

Galaxies spin with a giggle and whirl,
Planets play tag, giving stardust a twirl.
Black holes joke, 'We're just vacuuming space!'
While meteors race with a laugh and a chase.

Stars wear their shades, looking quite sly,
'Watch out for falling space pies!' they cry.
Gravity dances to a quirky tune,
As space critters jive under a laughing moon.

So raise a toast to the cosmos absurd,
Where laughter is cosmic, a universal word.
In this funny universe, nothing's too odd,
Join in the jest; it's a galactic facade!

Timeless Constellations

Up in the sky, the stars play a mix,
With squiggly patterns, they're up to their tricks.
The Big Dipper spills drinks on Orion's head,
While the Milky Way giggles at things we've said.

Old galaxies argue, who's the oldest of all?
While shooting stars laugh, they're ready to fall.
With laughter so bright, like stardust so fine,
These cosmic clowns know how to unwind.

Comets bring snacks, they're flying through space,
'Try these moon pies!', they cheer with a race.
Planetary pranks are the best in the night,
As satellites signal with beams of pure light.

So next time you gaze at the sky so wide,
Remember the fun that the stars cannot hide.
For timeless constellations hold tales full of glee,
In this vast, vivid universe, come laugh with me!

Between the Stars

Between the bright stars, the mischief unfolds,
Robots play chess while a spaceship scolds.
The moon throws a party; all planets invite,
Dancing with joy through the long, starry night.

Asteroids strum on their rock and roll guitars,
While space mice dance on the rings of bizarre.
Cosmic travelers drift with funny old maps,
Saying, 'We've hit a black hole, let's take a nap!'

Nebulas swirl in a colorful spree,
'They call me puffy; it's just how I be!'
Galaxies wink, flashing quirky designs,
Trading their stories like old friend rewinds.

So come join the fun, it's a whimsical flight,
Where laughter rings loud through the cosmos tonight.
Between sparkling stars, the giggles won't end,
In a universe filled with jest, we can blend!

Galactic Heartbeats

In the heart of the cosmos, there's a rhythm that plays,
Galactic heartbeats in curious ways.
Each planet pulsates with joy and delight,
While quarks and leptons dance through the night.

Stars share secrets, they twinkle and shine,
'This cosmic giggle? It's all by design!'
Supernovas burst, like fireworks bright,
While tiny black holes munch munch munch all night.

Planets parade with their rings all aglow,
Spinning in wonder, putting on quite a show.
Rocket ships zoom with a happy little beep,
Saying, 'Who said space is just dark and deep?'

So tap into the beat of the universe round,
There's laughter and joy in the leaps and the bounds.
In this cosmic tale, we all play a part,
Join in the fun, feel the beat of the heart!

Portraits of the Universe

In the sky, a chatty star,
Said to a comet, 'Look how far!'
With wigs of gas and tails of light,
They giggled through the endless night.

A black hole's joke went 'round the bend,
'What's your favorite shape, my friend?'
The planets laughed, they spun around,
'Circle us, we're glory-bound!'

Asteroids throw cosmic shade,
While aliens dance a silly parade.
'Watch your step!' a dwarf star warned,
As space shoes squeaked, the rhythm adorned.

Galaxies swoosh in rainbow hues,
While nebulae play peek-a-boo.
'In this vast, vast cosmic show,
Let's prance in orbits—whee! Let's go!'

Shadows of the Milky Way

Two stars chuckled, bright and bold,
'Who's the brightest? Should we fold?'
A shadow cast by floating dust,
'In my glow, can you see the must?'

Neutron shenanigans in the void,
Spinning tales that can't be buoyed.
'Hold my moon!' a gas giant yelled,
While comets fetched it, unrepelled.

Black holes squealed at gravitational pranks,
While orbiting moons formed silly ranks.
A wave of laughter swept through space,
'The universe is one big funny place!'

Andromeda winked, with a snide little grin,
'They think they won, but let the games begin!'
Twinkling bright with a mischievous flair,
Shadows dance with joy, in the endless air.

Celestial Encounters

A star met a planet, said, 'What a cute face!'
'We should hang out in this endless space!'
They spun in a tango, a meteor burst,
'Dance like nobody's watching, it's a cosmic thirst!'

Supernovae blushed, not quite sure how,
'We played too hard; should toe the line now?'
Galactic giggles filled the void wide,
As cosmos full of wonder turned the tide.

Aliens came with snacks in hand,
'Cosmic cuisine from the outer land!'
Asteroid chips and stardust dip,
The universe's finest, take a trip!

In this vast expanse, they all convened,
Where laughter echoed and dreams deemed.
'Stars unite!' proclaimed a voice so clear,
'Let's celebrate fun, it's our pioneer!'

Astral Connections

From Venus to Mars, a road trip planned,
With asteroids dancing in a stellar band.
'Pack the light-years, let's hit the trail!'
And bring some comets, we'll never fail!

Stardust sandwiches and moonbeam shakes,
Traveling fast, ignoring breaks.
Laughing wildly, passing by moons,
Waving hello to cosmic raccoons.

In endless space, they shared tall tales,
Of planets with thoughts and whispering gales.
'A black hole took my favorite sock!'
They rallied on, around the stellar clock.

'To infinity and beyond!' they all cheered,
With joy and laughter, no one feared.
Astral connections in the night so bright,
Creating laughter, a pure delight!

Tales from the Edge of Infinity

In a galaxy bright with tangled tales,
Aliens dance in rubbery veils.
They misplace their ships, oh what a sight,
Flying their saucers, they miss the flight.

With whoopee cushions to blast the mood,
Asteroids bouncing like a kid's food.
Cosmic pranks in the vast unknown,
They giggle and snicker, never alone.

Every black hole a portal of laughs,
Where space-time bends like silly staff.
A wormhole leads to a clown parade,
Interstellar giggles never fade.

From comets with mustaches, what a show,
Their trails of glitter all aglow.
So the stars chuckle with joy up high,
In the endless sky, where the funny fly.

Nebulous Hopes and Distant Yearnings

In a nebula swirling with cotton candy,
Aliens wish for a life that's dandy.
They shop for dreams at a cosmic fair,
Buying hope with a wink and a glare.

Cosmic doves deliver their mail,
Wrapped in stardust, they giggle and sail.
Shooting stars wish for pizza tonight,
As they zoom past the moon, what a sight.

Galaxies spin in hilarious jest,
Astrophysics, now part of the jest.
With a twist of humor, the cosmos plays,
In every odd corner, laughter stays.

So they'll toast with moons full of mirth,
To the wacky wonders of this vast Earth.
For amidst the chaos and nebulous dreams,
Lies a punchline hidden in cosmic beams.

Whispers of Stars in Silent Night

Chasing shadows of planets with cheer,
Stars send whispers for all to hear.
They sing the praises of socks and shoes,
In the silent night, they have fun to choose.

Planets juggle from left to right,
Spinning with laughter, oh what a sight!
Comets crack jokes as they fly around,
While asteroids dance on solid ground.

In the hush of night, jokes take flight,
With cosmic puns that tickle the light.
Saturn winks with its rings of gold,
Telling stories that never get old.

So amidst the stars, let laughter reign,
In the vastness of space, humor's the gain.
With every twinkle, a chuckle is cast,
In the universe, laughs are unsurpassed.

A Comet's Kiss Beneath Forgotten Skies

A comet winks with a sparkly grin,
Trail of giggles, a celestial spin.
It flirts with planets in dance so bright,
Oh what a spectacle in the night!

Stars taking bets on who'll catch a ride,
Planets bicker with humor applied.
In the backdrop of silence, joy erupts,
A cosmic circus where laughter erupts.

With each swing of asteroids, comedic flair,
The universe chuckles in lights and air.
Bright meteors flash with a playful jest,
Making the dark feel humorously blessed.

So let's toast to the comets that fly,
With kisses of laughter that never say goodbye.
In the tapestry woven in dusk and dawn,
The joy of the cosmos will never be gone.

Fragments of a Forgotten Galaxy

In a far-off realm, the stars do jest,
Quirky comets play, never take a rest.
Planets wobble in their cosmic dance,
While aliens giggle—what a strange romance!

Space junk floats by with a clatter and bang,
Asteroids chuckle at the songs we sang.
A black hole yawns, what a sight to see,
Swallowing whispers like it's tea-time, whee!

Galactic parties with guest stars galore,
Dancing light-years, we just want some more.
Jumping through wormholes, who knows where we land?

Laughter echoes through gravity's hand.

Fragments drift on, like confetti in air,
Tales of space silliness, fables we share.
In this cosmic circus, we're the merry few,
Exploring the vastness with a laugh or two.

Beyond the Event Horizon

Under the spotlight of a supernova's glow,
Floating with glee, the space travelers go.
Jokes tangle in beams of light beaming bright,
Wormhole wiggles make for a funny sight!

Past the horizon, where gravity whines,
Clumsy meteors tumble, crossing strange lines.
A rubber chicken lost in the stellar spree,
An intergalactic prank, oh what glee!

Stars in their pajamas, ready to sleep,
While black holes tease with secrets they keep.
Cosmic comedians twirl and they spin,
Telling tales of worlds where the laughter begins.

Far beyond time, where the cosmos advices,
Every giggle echoes as surprise rises.
In this laughter-filled journey, take heart and embrace,
For humor is timeless, a true cosmic grace.

Celestial Dancers

In the ballroom of space, where the oddballs sway,
Planets trade moves in their own silly way.
Shooting stars zoom, practicing for the show,
While space dust collects with a glittering glow.

Meteor showers slide by in a line,
Dressed up as rain, isn't that just divine?
Neutron stars spin, doing the twist,
Galactic goofballs making humor a tryst.

Asteroids tango, and asteroids waltz,
Each with a partner, no matter the faults.
In this cosmic gala, every step is a chance,
To giggle away as we move to the dance!

The Milky Way grins, with a wink in its eye,
As space takes a moment for laughter to sigh.
Join in the frolic, don't miss your cue,
For the universe dances—just waiting for you!

Stardust Reflections

In puddles of light, we see starlit grins,
Reflections of laughter, where the universe spins.
Galaxies mirror the jokes of the night,
Each twinkle a giggle, a shimmering delight.

Dust motes are winking, in cosmic ballet,
As planets exchange tales of their silliest day.
Comets, like jesters, dash by with a flash,
Leaving behind a trail of stardust and smash!

Black holes gossip about worlds they consume,
While nebulae chuckle in colorful plume.
The cosmos tickles, it sparks with delight,
Sending ripples of joy into the starry night.

So gather around, in this infinite sprawl,
Laugh with the cosmos, let your worries fall.
In stardust reflections, we'll find what we seek,
A universe smiling, cheeky and unique.

In the Shadow of Giants

In shadows where giants roam with ease,
Small creatures play and dance like bees,
They tiptoe 'round the cosmic laughs,
Building dreams from galactic drafts.

A comet sneezes, stars fall down,
Alien cows wear a cosmic crown,
They moo of wonders, past and near,
While asteroids laugh, they can't disappear.

A wormhole offers them a ride,
Spinning tales of the great wide glide,
With whimsy woven in every tale,
Their giggles echo in a starry gale.

So here they dance in cosmic cheer,
Playing tag with space, we hold dear,
In the shadows, they find their art,
Giggles and grins from the very start.

Navigating the Void

In a ship made of ice cream and dreams,
Navigators giggle and plot their schemes,
With maps drawn in chocolate, so sweet,
They steer through the stars with sticky feet.

A jellybean star blinks with delight,
As they chase candy comets in flight,
The vacuum's not dark, it's a soft purple hue,
With little green munchkins laughing too.

Asteroids wave as they drift by,
While space fish do the moonwalk nigh,
The void is a playground, full of repose,
Where laughter echoes like whimsical prose.

They dive through bubbles of cosmic gum,
Eating giggles, oh how they hum,
In this vast expanse of silly delight,
Navigating the void, all through the night.

When Stars Align

When stars align for a cosmic dance,
Aliens gather with joyful prance,
They don silly hats made of moonbeams,
Sharing their silliest, wildest dreams.

The sun winks, a cheeky little star,
Playing hide-and-seek, though not too far,
With giggles popping like popcorn bright,
They twirl and spin, caught in delight.

A disco ball of exploding sun,
Turns the sky into a party run,
Planets jump and through space, glide,
Embracing the rhythm with space as their guide.

So when stars align, don't miss the show,
Pour some stardust and let the good times flow,
With laughter as the soundtrack of night,
The universe joins in, feeling just right.

Encounters in the Cosmos

Little green friends from afar,
Trading jokes with a shooting star,
Spinning tales of their wacky days,
In a language of giggles, lost in the haze.

A nebula winks, paints the sky,
While space whales sing a lullaby,
Dancing through rings of Saturn's delight,
With giggles that echo through soft, starry nights.

They play hopscotch on asteroids round,
Laughing as gravity bounces them down,
In this cosmic playground, joy is the theme,
And every encounter feels like a dream.

So raise a toast with your cosmic glass,
To friendships that shine and never surpass,
In the great wide expanse, let's join the cheer,
For encounters in space, we hold so dear.

Boundless Skies and Celestial Holds

In a world where stars wear ties,
And comets glide in silly shoes,
Planets spin on cosmic swings,
While aliens take weird selfies too.

Jupiter juggles its moons with flair,
Saturn's rings hold a disco ball,
Mars plays tag with a space raccoon,
While laughter echoes through the hall.

Neptune's got a bubble bath,
Uranus just can't stop its giggles,
All the while, Earth tries to dance,
But trips over its own wiggles.

Asteroids throw a big confetti bash,
Shooting stars can't find their way,
Making wishes with a clumsy flash,
In the night sky's playful sway.

Constellations of Desire and Defiance

Orion's belt is a fashion show,
With stars parading in grand delight,
Every twinkle a bold fashion choice,
As they strut across the night.

Leo roars with a comedic tone,
While Virgo snags a cosmic date,
Yet Taurus starts a food fight spree,
With stardust snacks upon their plate.

Capricorn's climbing with a grin,
Pisces is juggling fish galore,
While the Gemini twins argue on,
About the best space pizza store.

Sagittarius always aims to please,
But knocks the planets out of place,
In this starry clash of laughter bright,
We find our joy in cosmic grace.

Hearts Intertwined in the Cosmos

Cupid's arrow shot through space,
Hit Mars but missed the rest,
Venus blushes in sheer surprise,
While Saturn's rings host a jest.

Black holes spin like tops so fast,
Pulling in love with a silly whirl,
And Milky Way's a chocolate treat,
Romancing every boy and girl.

Galaxies dance in a twinkling spree,
Underneath the watchful stars,
Where love can be an awkward joke,
And laughter echoes from afar.

In the cosmos, hearts collide,
With punchlines bright among the night,
As whims and wishes intertwine,
In this whimsical starlit sight.

The Gravity of Longing Under Distant Suns

Gravity is just a big old tease,
Pulling me closer, yet I float,
Under suns that twinkle and wink,
As if they know my hopes and hopes.

Stardust drifts like confetti bright,
While aliens hold a karaoke night,
Singing songs of love and fright,
In this space where dreams take flight.

Lightyears feel like a cosmic game,
Where distance only makes us grin,
And every wave from far-off stars,
Whispers sweetly, 'Come on in!'

Under the glow of distant spheres,
We shuffle through the cosmic fun,
In this universe of laughter loud,
Longing for love among the sun.

Tapestry of the Cosmos

In space where socks float free,
Asteroids dance just for me,
Galactic yarn spun in cheer,
Knitting stars, oh dear, oh dear.

A comet slips on cosmic ice,
Warping time in a game of dice,
Aliens laugh, their jokes quite crude,
While planets spin in silly moods.

Galaxies play tag at night,
Twinkling pranks, oh what a sight,
Gravity pulls but can't confine,
The cosmic giggle that's divine.

So let us weave our dreams so bright,
In this vast expanse of light,
With laughter echoing our way,
In the universe, we shall play.

Illuminated Pathways

On trails where starlight gleams,
Even black holes beam with dreams,
Shooting stars are pizza pies,
With toppings shaped as happy eyes.

Planets twirl in patterned hats,
As space cats chase after bats,
Navigating through a wink,
The universe loves to joke and blink.

Bouncing comets pass with flair,
Poking fun at all that's rare,
"Hey there, Earthlings, come join in!"
In this laughter, we all win.

With every glow and cosmic spark,
We wander through the cosmic park,
Where chuckles bounce from star to star,
In a universe that feels bizarre.

Starry-Eyed Wanderers

Wanderers in the starlit sea,
Laughing in zero gravity,
Chasing beams of light all day,
In galactic games we play.

Space whales sing to passing moons,
While asteroids tap funky tunes,
Jumping jellybeans drift on by,
In a cosmic dance, oh my, oh my.

Silly aliens share a drink,
While planets spin, they stop to blink,
"Catch me if you can," they tease,
Underneath the cosmic trees.

Embracing dreams on this grand spree,
Starry-eyes are wild and free,
With every giggle, we explore,
Wanderers in this cosmic lore.

Orbital Serenades

On orbits where the giggles flow,
Silly moons put on a show,
Twinkling lights in playful flight,
Bring smiles on this starlit night.

Neptune plays the ukulele strum,
While Mercury joins in with a drum,
Singing songs of cosmic cheer,
For every planet that draws near.

Dark matter spins with bold finesse,
Dancing in a cosmic dress,
Tickling comets as they go,
With a wink, a nod, and a glow.

So join us in this starry ride,
Where laughter echoes far and wide,
In orbital beams of joy we reign,
Savoring laughter like champagne.

The Language of Light

In the cosmos, I can see,
Starlight giggles, oh so free.
Aliens whisper in bright glow,
Words of love, they do bestow.

Comets race with tails so long,
Singing tunes, a cosmic song.
Planets twirl in a silly dance,
Making stars laugh at a glance.

Light beams bounce from here to there,
Joking round like they don't care.
In a galaxy full of cheer,
Bright banter rings, it's crystal clear.

So come along, take this ride,
In our ship, let dreams collide.
Together we can beam and shine,
With planetary jokes so divine.

Galactic Romance

In a nebula, we found our spark,
Dancing through the cosmic dark.
With green-skinned charm, you'd woo,
Over stardust, love so true.

Asteroids flirt with a playful wink,
In cosmic cafes, we sip and drink.
Martian snacks, they're quite a feat,
Together munching, oh so sweet!

Space whales croon a silly tune,
As we wink at the glowing moon.
Zooming past the Milky Way,
Your jokes make my day, hooray!

In this wild, galactic show,
Love's a dance, just so you know.
With every twirl, we spark delight,
A whimsical twist in starry night.

Dancing Through Space

Float with me on solar winds,
Where every giggle never ends.
Planets spin, they all take turns,
While starlit laughter brightly burns.

Aliens groove with floppy feet,
In zero-gravity, it's a treat.
Galaxies swirl in playful jest,
Join the fun; it's simply the best.

Asteroid cha-chas by my side,
While comets jiggle with great pride.
Cosmic boogies shake it right,
Dance away into the night!

Every pirouette a delight,
In this vast, enchanting flight.
So twirl with joy, let hearts embrace,
As we glide through boundless space.

Echoes of the Universe

In the void, where echoes play,
Galaxies joke, and stars sway.
Whispers swirl from here to Mars,
Sharing punchlines with the stars.

What did one black hole say to two?
'Why so serious? Just pull through!'
Cosmic giggles float on by,
With every laugh, the comets fly.

In the echoes, we find our way,
A luminous joke to save the day.
From supernovas, a hearty cheer,
Laughter ripples, crystal clear.

So hear the universe's tune,
As it dances round the moon.
Join the cosmic chuckle spree,
In the echoes, you'll find glee.

Celestial Journeys Between Worlds

In a rocket made of cheese,
We zoom past lunar bees.
Jupiter dances in a tutu,
While Saturn giggles, quite askew.

Martians offer moonlit pies,
As comets race to win the prize.
Alien tunes fill the air,
With wacky notes that twist and flare.

Stars wink from a velvet coat,
As we sail in our silly boat.
Galactic maps all upside down,
Navigating space in a clown's gown.

With wormholes as our twisting paths,
Our laughter sparks, igniting blasts.
A journey that's purely absurd,
Amongst the stars, we all concur!

Fading Light of Forgotten Galaxies

In twilight's glow, they begin to fade,
Where lost constellations once played.
Dusty comets dance, oh what a sight,
With no one to guide them, lost in flight.

Asteroids wearing funky hats,
Skip and hop like playful cats.
Whispers of supernovae laugh,
Reminding us of the cosmic gaffe.

Old black holes tell tales of yore,
Eating starlight like never before.
Their grins wide as they munch our dreams,
While light-years laugh in quirky themes.

Galaxies whisper in snickering tones,
As we drift past their rubbery bones.
In this twilight of the unseen,
Laughter fades, yet brightly gleams.

Passion's Echo in Void's Embrace

In the void, two stars collide,
With a giggle, they do glide.
Bright sparks fly, a love so vast,
As space-bound hearts beat fast.

Saturn sighs in shades of love,
As meteors dance and push and shove.
A cosmic flirt, with comets' tails,
Weave a tale of interstellar gales.

The moon sends winks in radiant beams,
Tickling the stars with silly dreams.
In this embrace of time and space,
Even black holes can find their place.

Fluttering through celestial fog,
In cosmic bars, they dance and jog.
An echo of passion's gentle tune,
Floating high, beneath a laughing moon.

Starlit Roads and Cosmic Connections

On starlit roads, we wander wide,
Where planets wave, no need to hide.
Cosmic maps scribbled in silly ink,
Guiding us as we stop to think.

Galaxies twirl in joyful spree,
Trading giggles, as we all agree.
A comet bar serves milkshake shakes,
While meteorites make splendid cakes.

Cosmic buddies in UFOs zoom,
Playing tag 'round the moons of gloom.
The universe hums a quirky tune,
As we dance and twirl through space's loom.

Connections made in laughter's glow,
As stars poke fun, putting on a show.
With each twist and twirl of delight,
We find our path, shining bright!

Luminescent Paths of Two Souls

In the glow of distant lights,
Two friends dance through cosmic nights.
They trip on space, they laugh and fall,
Who knew stardust could be a ball?

With silly hats and comets bright,
They zoom around like sprites in flight.
Galactic games and cosmic snacks,
In this wild universe, there are no lacks.

They chase the moons, they dodge the sun,
Twirl in orbit, oh what fun!
With each misstep, they jump and shout,
In this vast expanse, there's never doubt.

So here they go, on paths anew,
Two souls bright, as laughter grew.
They're luminescent, just like stars,
Together forever, despite the scars.

Beyond the Stars: An Unwritten Tale

In a ship made from old tin cans,
Two fools are heading for distant lands.
They steer with pizza, sip on cola,
Sketching tales like a cosmic loafer.

With every jump, they're filled with glee,
Racing meteors, oh can't you see?
They stumble, fall, and giggle loud,
A spectacle for the starry crowd.

Adventures written in stardust ink,
With quips so bright, they'll make you think.
In the void, their humor flies,
Creating laughter in the skies.

So, if you gaze into the night,
And catch a flicker or a light,
Know it's but two laughs unknown,
Beyond the stars, their tale is sown.

Timelines Collide in the Void

When past meets future, what a sight!
Two bumpy timelines taking flight.
They burst through time, hiccup and twirl,
In a wobbly dance, they laugh and whirl.

One wears a hat from days of yore,
The other sports tech from a future score.
They bicker and jest, all in good fun,
Silly debates on who's the 'one.'

In the vastness, they stumble, collide,
Chasing dreams on a cosmic ride.
With every hiccup, more jokes arise,
In this grand mix-up, they're the prize.

So here they wade in temporal streams,
Shooting past histories, living their dreams.
Through the chaos, a slapstick play,
In the void of time, they'll forever stay.

Celestial Bonds and Cosmic Caresses

In the cradle of the stars so bright,
Two pals share giggles, oh what a sight!
A whirling galaxy of goofy grace,
With silly smiles on each bright face.

They toss around moons like soft balloons,
Dancing to the rhythm of bouncing tunes.
With cosmic sprinkles on their cake,
What other chaos can they make?

Through meteor showers and asteroids,
They celebrate with laughter and no voids.
In this tapestry of space's embrace,
They find the joy, and love's sweet trace.

So if you glimpse those twinkling lights,
Know it's two souls sharing cosmic sights.
Their bond is stronger than any star,
In perfect chaos, they'll never spar.

Threads of Time and Space

In galaxies far, a ship went awry,
With aliens waving, oh my, oh my!
They toasted with pizza, instead of a drink,
And danced on the stars, what a sight to think!

Warp drives malfunctioned, they spun like a top,
While robots were zipping, they couldn't quite stop.
A cosmic spaghetti on a plate floating near,
Who knew space travel could end in such cheer?

They charted a course through a comet of cheese,
While giggling at jokes with intergalactic ease.
With wormholes as bridges, and stars as their guide,
In the universe's playground, wild they would ride!

So next time you gaze at the night sky so bold,
Remember the pirates trading laughter for gold.
Threads of time and space spun in a jest,
In the funny old cosmos, we're all just a guest.

Luminous Horizons

A flicker of light from a distant sun's wink,
An astronaut tripped on a star's cosmic link.
With a grin like a moonbeam, he ventured out wide,
Tumbling through space on a glittery slide!

The planets all chuckled, what a sight to behold,
As rockets became sailboats, bold tales left untold.
With Martian friends building a house made of rock,
And Earthlings debating the best moonlit cock!

Meteors raced in a dizzying dance,
While aliens cheered from their odd little trance.
A carnival sparkled in a nebula's hue,
Where laughter was universal and skies never blue!

So lift up your eyes to horizons aglow,
And laugh like the cosmos, let your spirits grow.
In this zany adventure, with stars in our sight,
The universe chuckles, bathed in pure light.

Celestial Choreography

Planets are dancing in a grand old ballet,
With comets as pirouettes, swirling in play.
The sun leads the charge, in a dazzling show,
While moons trip and stumble, putting on a glow!

Neptune lost his shoe on the rings of a star,
While Jupiter laughed, rocking out on guitar.
They twirled through the stardust, no worries around,
As black holes did twirl, stealing glances profound!

A cosmic conga line stretched far and wide,
With aliens shimmying alongside the tide.
Galaxies giggling, spinning out of sight,
In this waltz of the heavens, everything feels right!

So join in this dance, let your troubles take flight,
In the cosmic ballroom, there's joy every night.
Celestial choreography, laughter to embrace,
Together we twirl through the vastness of space.

Harmonies of the Heavens

With starlight composing, a concert takes stage,
Bad puns from the asteroids, the crowd in a rage.
A symphony bright, with sounds of delight,
As aliens harmonized under the moonlight!

Uranus sang low, while Venus was high,
Saturn played piano, the notes reaching the sky.
They jammed with abandon, forgetting their plans,
As meteors clapped their tiny little hands!

Mars brought the rhythm with a drum made of dust,
And Earth sang the blues, because singing's a must.
The Milky Way sparkled, the crowd cheered with glee,
In the grand cosmic lounge, we danced wild and free!

So raise up your voice, in this cosmic parade,
With harmonies ringing, let worries all fade.
In the vastness of night, let laughter ignite,
In the harmony of heavens, everything's right!

A Dance with the Cosmos

In the garden of stars, we twirl and spin,
Galaxies laugh, let the party begin!
With comets as confetti, we dance 'til dawn,
Even black holes are grooving, come on, come on!

Martians bring snacks, space worms on a plate,
Jupiter's moons say, "This party's first-rate!"
We share silly jokes with a wink and a grin,
As nebulae giggle, where do I begin?

The Milky Way chorus sings out a tune,
While shooting stars flash like a bright disco moon.
Astronauts join in, they can't help but sway,
In this cosmic carnival, we dance all day!

So here's to our friends, in the void up above,
Where laughter and stardust mix freely with love.
As we waltz through the galaxies, hand in hand,
In this cheerful cosmos, forever we'll stand!

Interstellar Dreams

Floating in dreams, on a pillow of light,
Planets play hopscotch, oh what a sight!
Saturn's found giggles in its ring's embrace,
While a meteor shower shows off its grace.

Starships like fish swim in a liquid sky,
With alien kids tossing shadowy pie.
The sun takes a dip, just to make a splash,
While Venus flips pancakes with a cosmic thrash.

Orion is searching for his lost space shoe,
While comets compete in a game of peekaboo.
Through planets and starlit dreams, we glide,
With laughter and joy, our dreams as our guide.

So toss out your worries, let your spirits soar,
In a universe bursting with wonders in store.
With every heartbeat, we'll dance through the night,
In our interstellar dreams, everything feels right!

Beloved in the Cosmos

Oh, my sweet universe, how you twinkle and tease,
With quirks in your laughter like a cosmic breeze.
Each star a dancer in a vast ballroom bright,
With winks and nods, they're our joy and delight.

Neptune's got jokes that are deep as the sea,
While Pluto keeps secrets, but shares them with me.
Together we frolic through asteroid fields,
In this grand cosmic playground, love never yields.

Stars paint the sky with their cheerful hues,
As we spin through the cosmos, sharing our views.
With every twirl, there's a story to share,
In this boundless expanse, oh, how we care!

So here in the void, let's giggle and sing,
With planets aligning, joy is our king.
In the heart of the cosmos, together we roam,
Beloved in starlight, forever our home!

Lament of the Distant Stars

Alas, the stars cry in a comical way,
With twinkling laughs that brighten our day.
Wishing on wishes, but they trip and fall,
While aliens chuckle at the cosmic brawl.

In distant realms where the light travels fast,
The galaxies giggle at moments on blast.
While supernovae burst like fireworks bright,
The stars throw a party, oh, what a sight!

A black hole mutters, "I just lost my hat!"
While space dust dances in a playful spat.
With laughter echoing through the void so wide,
These celestial jesters take joy in their ride.

So let's raise a toast to the stars up high,
Who spin tales of whimsy as we pass by.
In the grand cosmic play, their laughter's the key,
For in humor and joy, forever we'll be!

Messages from the Cosmos

In the night sky, a joke is told,
Stars giggle softly, bright and bold.
Planets spin in a silly dance,
Comets wink, giving joy a chance.

Aliens watch with popcorn in hand,
Laughing at humans, so poorly planned.
Whispers from Venus, a cosmic prank,
Sending signals, watch your tank!

Lost in space, with too much to do,
Stumbling through galaxies, just like you.
Martians mime, pull off silly tricks,
While Saturn's rings are used for kicks.

So next time you look up and see,
Remember the universe loves to be free.
Cosmic laughter is all in good fun,
Just a reminder: you're not the only one!

Cosmic Tides

Waves of stardust wash ashore,
Galactic bubbles, who could ask for more?
Jupiter's storms are just wind-up toys,
While space whales play with cosmic noise.

Gravity pulls, but not as a friend,
It fakes a hug, then it will bend.
Nebulas swirl like a swirling cone,
Making ice cream scoops in a galaxy known.

The Milky Way's a wild dance floor,
Jiving with meteors, hear them roar!
Cosmic tides, they ebb and flow,
While stars giggle, "Hey, look at that glow!"

So surf those beams through the stellar night,
With a laugh and a joke, take flight!
The universe smiles, tickles the spine,
In cosmic rhythms, we're all just fine.

Star-Crossed Journeys

Two stars met on a date gone wrong,
One was too bright, the other too long.
Laughing, they spun, creating a mess,
With comets swooping in to redress.

Across the Milky Way, they roamed,
Dodging black holes, feeling un-homed.
"Hey, watch that asteroid!" they both yelled,
As flying space junk was swiftly dispelled.

Through supernovae, their laughter soared,
While aliens clapped, utterly floored.
Star-crossed paths twist like a wild vine,
In this galaxy, love's truly divine!

So next time you see a flash on high,
Remember those stars that gave it a try.
They're out there giggling, still on a spree,
In celestial corners, just you and me!

Infinity's Embrace

In the arms of starlight, laughter murmurs,
Planets hug tightly, circling like spinners.
A cosmic embrace, where time takes a break,
And wormholes giggle, for fun's own sake.

Black holes play tag with runaway gas,
While light beams dance and twirl as they pass.
Gravity giggles, a mischievous grin,
Pulling stars closer, letting the fun begin.

Endless horizons of twinkling delight,
With meteors splashing like stars in a fight.
Infinity's close, it's not what it seems,
Just a universe filled with whimsical dreams!

So float through the cosmos, rejoice in the jam,
With laughter that echoes, a universal slam.
Together we spin, in this vast, silly space,
In infinity's embrace, we find our place!

Starlit Whispers of a Distant Dream

In a galaxy far, they dined on blue cheese,
With aliens giggling, all aiming to please.
Between hiccups and laughs, they shared space pies,
As stars winked above, twinkling with sighs.

Jupiter's moon played hide-and-seek games,
While Martians drew pictures with odd, silly names.
Beneath cosmic arches, they twirled with delight,
Time zipped by fast in the soft, starry night.

Comets zoomed by with a cheer and a grin,
While Saturn folks danced with their rings made of tin.
Giggles and winks in that stellar parade,
As stardust-filled dreams began to cascade.

A telescope peeped, and the laughter ran free,
"Come find me!" they yelled, hiding deep in a tree.
With starlit confetti, they laughed in a blur,
In the zany night sky where chaos would stir.

Celestial Secrets and Cosmic Hearts

A spaceship zoomed past, fueled by cupcakes,
As alien pilots devised sneaky pranks.
Among glowing asteroids, jokes were exchanged,
With each playful pun, the universe changed.

Planetary beings in pajamas of red,
Told stories of worlds where gravity fled.
With giggles like quasars, their laughter would ring,
As meteors danced in a cosmic ring.

Unicorns rode comets, their manes all aglow,
While star dragons sucked on a milkshake flow.
In the heart of a nebula, all could see,
It's fun being odd in the expanse of the spree!

Over cosmic pancakes, they toasted with glee,
"Here's to bizarre beams of oddity!"
With laughter as fuel, they soared through the night,
In sparkles and joy, everything felt right.

Echoes from a Galactic Embrace

On a distant planet, they played hide and seek,
With beans that giggled and pizza that spoke.
Each orbit a laugh, each moon a new game,
In that spiraled embrace of fun without shame.

Extraterrestrials all tossed around pies,
While Grandmas of Saturn baked gooey surprise.
With confetti-like stars that fell from the skies,
They cheered as the galaxy spun with their sighs.

Puppies made of stardust chased tails made of light,
As galaxies twinkled, filling all hearts with delight.
With whimsical winks, they tickled each star,
In a cosmic cacophony, they laughed from afar.

A rocket ship zoomed by with a squeaky toy sound,
In the dance of the cosmos, pure silliness found.
With echoes of humor, love twinkled and played,
In an eternal embrace, laughter surely stayed.

Threads of Time in Nebulae's Haze

Weaving through nebulae, time took a spin,
With lilies like laughter and giggles within.
Past black holes that burped, there was much to explore,
As beams of bright humor popped out for more.

Galaxies twirled in a tango of fun,
While comets threw glitter like confetti to run.
Starships with capes soared on breezy night sails,
As laughter and joy painted bright, glowing trails.

With cupcakes of stardust and jellybean hue,
They melted their worries, while dreaming anew.
In the haze of the cosmos, shenanigans thrived,
Where laughter is time, and joy is alive.

So raise up your glasses made of moonbeam light,
Let's toast to the giggles and dance with delight!
For in this vast universe, we're all just a part,
Of the thread that weaves laughter, a cosmic sweet heart.

www.ingramcontent.com/pod-product-compliance
Lightning Source LLC
Chambersburg PA
CBHW051700160426
43209CB00004B/969